My Digital Media Journal

Capture and document your notes from Digital Media sources like Online Videos, Webinars, Podcasts, and more, in an organized and reflective way

TABLE OF CONTENTS

CATEGORY 1

Title:

Page   *Content / Video Title:*

Page: *Content / Video Title:*

Page: *Content / Video Title:*

Page: *Content / Video Title:*

Page: *Content / Video Title:*

Page: *Content / Video Title:*

Page: *Content / Video Title:*

Page: *Content / Video Title:*

Page: *Content / Video Title:*

Page: *Content / Video Title:*

Page: *Content / Video Title:*

Page: *Content / Video Title:*

Page: *Content / Video Title:*

Page: *Content / Video Title:*

CATEGORY 2

CATEGORY 3

Title:

Page   *Content / Video Title:*

Page: *Content / Video Title:*

Page: *Content / Video Title:*

Page: *Content / Video Title:*

Page: *Content / Video Title:*

Page: *Content / Video Title:*

Page: *Content / Video Title:*

Page: *Content / Video Title:*

Page: *Content / Video Title:*

Page: *Content / Video Title:*

Page: *Content / Video Title:*

Page: *Content / Video Title:*

Page: *Content / Video Title:*

Page: *Content / Video Title:*

CATEGORY 4

CATEGORY 1

CATEGORY: Date:

Title :

Publisher / Creator :

Website / URL :

Duration: hour(s):   minute(s):

Timestamp	Takeaway 1
:	

Timestamp	Takeaway 2
:	

Timestamp	Takeaway 3
:	

Reflection / Note:

How did the video impact you?

Did it spark any ideas?

Rating

☆ ☆ ☆ ☆ ☆

CATEGORY: Date:

Title :

Publisher / Creator :

Website / URL :

Duration: hour(s):   minute(s):

Timestamp	Takeaway 1
:	

Timestamp	Takeaway 2
:	

Timestamp	Takeaway 3
:	

Reflection / Note:

How did the video impact you?

Did it spark any ideas?

Rating

☆ ☆ ☆ ☆ ☆

Timestamp
Takeaway

Timestamp
Takeaway

Timestamp
Takeaway

Timestamp
Takeaway

Timestamp
Takeaway

Timestamp
Takeaway

CATEGORY: Date:

Title :

Publisher / Creator :

Website / URL :

Duration: hour(s):   minute(s):

Timestamp

:

Takeaway 1

Timestamp

:

Takeaway 2

Timestamp

:

Takeaway 3

Reflection / Note:

How did the video impact you?

Did it spark any ideas?

Rating

☆ ☆ ☆ ☆ ☆

Timestamp	Takeaway
:	

Timestamp	Takeaway
:	

Timestamp	Takeaway
:	

Timestamp	Takeaway
:	

Timestamp	Takeaway
:	

Timestamp	Takeaway
:	

CATEGORY: Date:

Duration: hour(s):   minute(s):

Timestamp	Takeaway 1
:	

Timestamp	Takeaway 2
:	

Timestamp	Takeaway 3
:	

Reflection / Note:

How did the video impact you?

Did it spark any ideas?

Rating

☆ ☆ ☆ ☆ ☆

Timestamp	Takeaway
:	
Timestamp	Takeaway
:	
Timestamp	Takeaway
:	
Timestamp	Takeaway
:	
Timestamp	Takeaway
:	
Timestamp	Takeaway
:	

CATEGORY: Date:

Title :

Publisher / Creator :

Website / URL :

Duration: hour(s):   minute(s):

Timestamp	Takeaway 1
:	

Timestamp	Takeaway 2
:	

Timestamp	Takeaway 3
:	

Reflection / Note:

How did the video impact you?

Did it spark any ideas?

Rating

☆ ☆ ☆ ☆ ☆

Timestamp	Takeaway
:	
:	
:	
:	
:	
:	

CATEGORY: Date:

Title :

Publisher / Creator :

Website / URL :

Duration: hour(s):   minute(s):

Timestamp	Takeaway 1
:	

Timestamp	Takeaway 2
:	

Timestamp	Takeaway 3
:	

Reflection / Note:

How did the video impact you?

Did it spark any ideas?

Rating

☆ ☆ ☆ ☆ ☆

Timestamp	Takeaway
:	

Timestamp	Takeaway
:	

Timestamp	Takeaway
:	

Timestamp	Takeaway
:	

Timestamp	Takeaway
:	

Timestamp	Takeaway
:	

CATEGORY: Date:

Title :

Publisher / Creator :

Website / URL :

Duration: hour(s):   minute(s):

Timestamp	Takeaway 1
:	

Timestamp	Takeaway 2
:	

Timestamp	Takeaway 3
:	

Reflection / Note:

How did the video impact you?

Did it spark any ideas?

Rating

☆ ☆ ☆ ☆ ☆

Timestamp	Takeaway
:	
:	
:	
:	
:	
:	

CATEGORY: Date:

| Title : |
| Publisher / Creator : |
| Website / URL : |

Duration: hour(s):   minute(s):

| Timestamp | Takeaway 1 |
| : | |

| Timestamp | Takeaway 2 |
| : | |

| Timestamp | Takeaway 3 |
| : | |

Reflection / Note:

How did the video impact you?

Did it spark any ideas?

Rating

☆ ☆ ☆ ☆ ☆

Timestamp
Takeaway

Timestamp
Takeaway

Timestamp
Takeaway

Timestamp
Takeaway

Timestamp
Takeaway

Timestamp
Takeaway

CATEGORY: Date:

Title :

Publisher / Creator :

Website / URL :

Duration: hour(s):   minute(s):

Timestamp	Takeaway 1
:	

Timestamp	Takeaway 2
:	

Timestamp	Takeaway 3
:	

Reflection / Note:

How did the video impact you?

Did it spark any ideas?

Rating

☆ ☆ ☆ ☆ ☆

Timestamp
Takeaway

:

Timestamp
Takeaway

:

Timestamp
Takeaway

:

Timestamp
Takeaway

:

Timestamp
Takeaway

:

Timestamp
Takeaway

:

CATEGORY: Date:

Title :

Publisher / Creator :

Website / URL :

Duration: hour(s):   minute(s):

Timestamp	Takeaway 1
:	

Timestamp	Takeaway 2
:	

Timestamp	Takeaway 3
:	

Reflection / Note:

How did the video impact you?

Did it spark any ideas?

Rating

☆ ☆ ☆ ☆ ☆

Timestamp	Takeaway
:	
:	
:	
:	
:	
:	

CATEGORY: Date:

Title :

Publisher / Creator :

Website / URL :

Duration: hour(s):   minute(s):

Timestamp	Takeaway 1
:	

Timestamp	Takeaway 2
:	

Timestamp	Takeaway 3
:	

Reflection / Note:

How did the video impact you?

Did it spark any ideas?

Rating

☆ ☆ ☆ ☆ ☆

CATEGORY: Date:

Title :	
Publisher / Creator :	
Website / URL :	

Duration: hour(s):   minute(s):

| Timestamp | Takeaway 1 |
| : | |

| Timestamp | Takeaway 2 |
| : | |

| Timestamp | Takeaway 3 |
| : | |

Reflection / Note:

How did the video impact you?

Did it spark any ideas?

Rating

☆ ☆ ☆ ☆ ☆

CATEGORY: Date:

Title :

Publisher / Creator :

Website / URL :

Duration: hour(s):   minute(s):

Timestamp	Takeaway 1
:	

Timestamp	Takeaway 2
:	

Timestamp	Takeaway 3
:	

Reflection / Note:

How did the video impact you?

Did it spark any ideas?

Rating

☆ ☆ ☆ ☆ ☆

Timestamp
Takeaway
:
Timestamp
Takeaway
:
Timestamp
Takeaway
:
Timestamp
Takeaway
:
Timestamp
Takeaway
:
Timestamp
Takeaway
:

CATEGORY: Date:

Title:

Publisher / Creator:

Website / URL:

Duration: hour(s):   minute(s):

Timestamp	Takeaway 1
:	

Timestamp	Takeaway 2
:	

Timestamp	Takeaway 3
:	

Reflection / Note:

How did the video impact you?

Did it spark any ideas?

Rating

☆ ☆ ☆ ☆ ☆

Timestamp	Takeaway
:	
:	
:	
:	
:	
:	

CATEGORY: Date:

Title :

Publisher / Creator :

Website / URL :

Duration: hour(s):   minute(s):

Timestamp   Takeaway 1

:

Timestamp   Takeaway 2

:

Timestamp   Takeaway 3

:

Reflection / Note:

How did the video impact you?

Did it spark any ideas?

Rating
☆ ☆ ☆ ☆ ☆

Timestamp	Takeaway
:	

Timestamp	Takeaway
:	

Timestamp	Takeaway
:	

Timestamp	Takeaway
:	

Timestamp	Takeaway
:	

Timestamp	Takeaway
:	

2
CATEGORY

CATEGORY: Date:

Title :

Publisher / Creator :

Website / URL :

Duration: hour(s):   minute(s):

Timestamp	Takeaway 1
:	

Timestamp	Takeaway 2
:	

Timestamp	Takeaway 3
:	

Reflection / Note:

How did the video impact you?

Did it spark any ideas?

Rating

Timestamp	Takeaway
:	
:	
:	
:	
:	
:	

CATEGORY: Date:

Title :

Publisher / Creator :

Website / URL :

Duration: hour(s):   minute(s):

Timestamp	Takeaway 1
:	

Timestamp	Takeaway 2
:	

Timestamp	Takeaway 3
:	

Reflection / Note:

How did the video impact you?

Did it spark any ideas?

Rating

☆ ☆ ☆ ☆ ☆

Timestamp

Takeaway

:

Timestamp

Takeaway

:

Timestamp

Takeaway

:

Timestamp

Takeaway

:

Timestamp

Takeaway

:

Timestamp

Takeaway

:

CATEGORY: Date:

Title :

Publisher / Creator :

Website / URL :

Duration: hour(s):   minute(s):

Timestamp	Takeaway 1
:	

Timestamp	Takeaway 2
:	

Timestamp	Takeaway 3
:	

Reflection / Note:

How did the video impact you?

Did it spark any ideas?

Rating

   ☆ ☆

Timestamp	Takeaway
:	

Timestamp	Takeaway
:	

Timestamp	Takeaway
:	

Timestamp	Takeaway
:	

Timestamp	Takeaway
:	

Timestamp	Takeaway
:	

CATEGORY: Date:

Title :

Publisher / Creator :

Website / URL :

Duration: hour(s):   minute(s):

Timestamp	Takeaway 1

Timestamp	Takeaway 2

Timestamp	Takeaway 3

Reflection / Note:

How did the video impact you?

Did it spark any ideas?

Rating

☆ ☆ ☆ ☆ ☆

Timestamp	Takeaway
:	

Timestamp	Takeaway
:	

Timestamp	Takeaway
:	

Timestamp	Takeaway
:	

Timestamp	Takeaway
:	

Timestamp	Takeaway
:	

CATEGORY: Date:

Duration: hour(s):   minute(s):

Timestamp	Takeaway 1
:	

Timestamp	Takeaway 2
:	

Timestamp	Takeaway 3
:	

Reflection / Note:

How did the video impact you?

Did it spark any ideas?

Rating

  ☆ ☆ ☆ ☆ ☆

Timestamp
Takeaway
:

Timestamp
Takeaway
:

Timestamp
Takeaway
:

Timestamp
Takeaway
:

Timestamp
Takeaway
:

Timestamp
Takeaway
:

CATEGORY: Date:

Title :

Publisher / Creator :

Website / URL :

Duration: hour(s):   minute(s):

Timestamp	Takeaway 1
:	

Timestamp	Takeaway 2
:	

Timestamp	Takeaway 3
:	

Reflection / Note:

How did the video impact you?

Did it spark any ideas?

Rating

☆ ☆ ☆ ☆ ☆

Timestamp	Takeaway
:	
:	
:	
:	
:	
:	

CATEGORY: Date:

Title :

Publisher / Creator :

Website / URL :

Duration: hour(s):   minute(s):

Timestamp	Takeaway 1
:	

Timestamp	Takeaway 2
:	

Timestamp	Takeaway 3
:	

Reflection / Note:

How did the video impact you?

Did it spark any ideas?

Rating

☆ ☆ ☆ ☆ ☆

Timestamp	Takeaway
:	
:	
:	
:	
:	
:	

CATEGORY: Date:

Title :

Publisher / Creator :

Website / URL :

Duration: hour(s):   minute(s):

Timestamp	Takeaway 1
:	

Timestamp	Takeaway 2
:	

Timestamp	Takeaway 3
:	

Reflection / Note:

How did the video impact you?

Did it spark any ideas?

Rating

☆ ☆ ☆ ☆ ☆

Timestamp
Takeaway
:

Timestamp
Takeaway
:

Timestamp
Takeaway
:

Timestamp
Takeaway
:

Timestamp
Takeaway
:

Timestamp
Takeaway
:

CATEGORY: Date:

Duration: hour(s):   minute(s):

Timestamp	Takeaway 1
:	

Timestamp	Takeaway 2
:	

Timestamp	Takeaway 3
:	

Reflection / Note:

How did the video impact you?

Did it spark any ideas?

Rating

☆ ☆ ☆ ☆ ☆

Timestamp	Takeaway
:	
Timestamp	Takeaway
:	
Timestamp	Takeaway
:	
Timestamp	Takeaway
:	
Timestamp	Takeaway
:	
Timestamp	Takeaway
:	

CATEGORY: Date:

Title :

Publisher / Creator :

Website / URL :

Duration: hour(s):   minute(s):

Timestamp	Takeaway 1
:	

Timestamp	Takeaway 2
:	

Timestamp	Takeaway 3
:	

Reflection / Note:

How did the video impact you?

Did it spark any ideas?

Rating

☆ ☆ ☆ ☆ ☆

Timestamp	Takeaway
:	
:	
:	
:	
:	
:	

CATEGORY: Date:

Duration: hour(s):   minute(s):

Timestamp	Takeaway 1

Timestamp	Takeaway 2

Timestamp	Takeaway 3

Reflection / Note:

How did the video impact you?

Did it spark any ideas?

Rating

Timestamp	Takeaway
:	

Timestamp	Takeaway
:	

Timestamp	Takeaway
:	

Timestamp	Takeaway
:	

Timestamp	Takeaway
:	

Timestamp	Takeaway
:	

CATEGORY: Date:

Title :

Publisher / Creator :

Website / URL :

Duration: hour(s):   minute(s):

Timestamp	Takeaway 1
:	

Timestamp	Takeaway 2
:	

Timestamp	Takeaway 3
:	

Reflection / Note:

How did the video impact you?

Did it spark any ideas?

Rating

☆ ☆ ☆ ☆ ☆

Timestamp	Takeaway
:	
:	
:	
:	
:	
:	

CATEGORY: Date:

Title :

Publisher / Creator :

Website / URL :

Duration: hour(s):   minute(s):

Timestamp	**Takeaway 1**
:	

Timestamp	**Takeaway 2**
:	

Timestamp	**Takeaway 3**
:	

Reflection / Note:

How did the video impact you?

Did it spark any ideas?

Rating

☆ ☆ ☆ ☆ ☆

Timestamp
Takeaway
Timestamp
Takeaway
Timestamp
Takeaway
Timestamp
Takeaway
Timestamp
Takeaway
Timestamp
Takeaway

CATEGORY: Date:

Duration: hour(s):   minute(s):

Timestamp	Takeaway 1
:	

Timestamp	Takeaway 2
:	

Timestamp	Takeaway 3
:	

Reflection / Note:

How did the video impact you?

Did it spark any ideas?

Rating

☆ ☆ ☆ ☆ ☆

Timestamp	Takeaway
:	

Timestamp	Takeaway
:	

Timestamp	Takeaway
:	

Timestamp	Takeaway
:	

Timestamp	Takeaway
:	

Timestamp	Takeaway
:	

CATEGORY: Date:

Title :
Publisher / Creator :
Website / URL :

Duration: hour(s):   minute(s):

Timestamp	Takeaway 1
:	

Timestamp	Takeaway 2
:	

Timestamp	Takeaway 3
:	

Reflection / Note:

How did the video impact you?

Did it spark any ideas?

Rating

☆ ☆ ☆ ☆ ☆

Timestamp	Takeaway
:	
:	
:	
:	
:	
:	

3
CATEGORY

CATEGORY: Date:

Title :

Publisher / Creator :

Website / URL :

Duration: hour(s):   minute(s):

Timestamp	Takeaway 1

Timestamp	Takeaway 2

Timestamp	Takeaway 3

Reflection / Note:

How did the video impact you?

Did it spark any ideas?

Rating

☆ ☆ ☆ ☆ ☆

Timestamp
Takeaway
:

Timestamp
Takeaway
:

Timestamp
Takeaway
:

Timestamp
Takeaway
:

Timestamp
Takeaway
:

Timestamp
Takeaway
:

CATEGORY: Date:

| Title : |
| Publisher / Creator : |
| Website / URL : |

Duration: hour(s):   minute(s):

| Timestamp | Takeaway 1 |

| Timestamp | Takeaway 2 |

| Timestamp | Takeaway 3 |

Reflection / Note:

How did the video impact you?

Did it spark any ideas?

Rating

☆ ☆ ☆ ☆ ☆

Timestamp	Takeaway
:	
:	
:	
:	
:	
:	

CATEGORY: Date:

Title :

Publisher / Creator :

Website / URL :

Duration: hour(s):   minute(s):

Timestamp	Takeaway 1

Timestamp	Takeaway 2

Timestamp	Takeaway 3

Reflection / Note:

How did the video impact you?

Did it spark any ideas?

Rating

☆ ☆ ☆ ☆ ☆

Timestamp	Takeaway
:	
:	
:	
:	
:	
:	

Title :

Publisher / Creator :

Website / URL :

Duration:　　　hour(s):　　　minute(s):

Timestamp	Takeaway 1
:	

Timestamp	Takeaway 2
:	

Timestamp	Takeaway 3
:	

Reflection / Note:

How did the video impact you?

Did it spark any ideas?

Rating

☆ ☆ ☆ ☆ ☆

CATEGORY: Date:

| Title : |
| Publisher / Creator : |
| Website / URL : |

Duration: hour(s):   minute(s):

| Timestamp | Takeaway 1 |
| : | |

| Timestamp | Takeaway 2 |
| : | |

| Timestamp | Takeaway 3 |
| : | |

Reflection / Note:

How did the video impact you?

Did it spark any ideas?

Rating

☆ ☆ ☆ ☆ ☆

Timestamp	Takeaway
:	

Timestamp	Takeaway
:	

Timestamp	Takeaway
:	

Timestamp	Takeaway
:	

Timestamp	Takeaway
:	

Timestamp	Takeaway
:	

CATEGORY: Date:

Title :

Publisher / Creator :

Website / URL :

Duration: hour(s):   minute(s):

Timestamp   Takeaway 1

:

Timestamp   Takeaway 2

:

Timestamp   Takeaway 3

:

Reflection / Note:

How did the video impact you?

Did it spark any ideas?

Rating

☆ ☆ ☆ ☆ ☆

Timestamp	Takeaway
:	
:	
:	
:	
:	
:	

CATEGORY: Date:

Title :

Publisher / Creator :

Website / URL :

Duration: hour(s):   minute(s):

Timestamp	Takeaway 1
:	

Timestamp	Takeaway 2
:	

Timestamp	Takeaway 3
:	

Reflection / Note:

How did the video impact you?

Did it spark any ideas?

Rating

☆ ☆ ☆ ☆ ☆

Timestamp	Takeaway
:	
:	
:	
:	
:	
:	

CATEGORY: Date:

| Title : |
| Publisher / Creator : |
| Website / URL : |

Duration: hour(s):   minute(s):

| Timestamp | Takeaway 1 |
| : | |

| Timestamp | Takeaway 2 |
| : | |

| Timestamp | Takeaway 3 |
| : | |

Reflection / Note:

How did the video impact you?

Did it spark any ideas?

Rating

☆ ☆ ☆ ☆ ☆

Timestamp	Takeaway
:	
:	
:	
:	
:	
:	

CATEGORY: Date:

Title :

Publisher / Creator :

Website / URL :

Duration: hour(s):   minute(s):

Timestamp	Takeaway 1
:	

Timestamp	Takeaway 2
:	

Timestamp	Takeaway 3
:	

Reflection / Note:

How did the video impact you?

Did it spark any ideas?

Rating

☆ ☆ ☆ ☆ ☆

Timestamp	Takeaway
:	

Timestamp	Takeaway
:	

Timestamp	Takeaway
:	

Timestamp	Takeaway
:	

Timestamp	Takeaway
:	

Timestamp	Takeaway
:	

CATEGORY: Date:

Title :

Publisher / Creator :

Website / URL :

Duration: hour(s):   minute(s):

Timestamp	Takeaway 1
:	

Timestamp	Takeaway 2
:	

Timestamp	Takeaway 3
:	

Reflection / Note:

How did the video impact you?

Did it spark any ideas?

Rating

☆ ☆ ☆ ☆ ☆

Timestamp
Takeaway
:

Timestamp
Takeaway
:

Timestamp
Takeaway
:

Timestamp
Takeaway
:

Timestamp
Takeaway
:

Timestamp
Takeaway
:

CATEGORY: Date:

Title :

Publisher / Creator :

Website / URL :

Duration: hour(s):   minute(s):

Timestamp	Takeaway 1
:	

Timestamp	Takeaway 2
:	

Timestamp	Takeaway 3
:	

Reflection / Note:

How did the video impact you?

Did it spark any ideas?

Rating

☆ ☆ ☆ ☆ ☆

Timestamp	Takeaway
:	
:	
:	
:	
:	
:	

CATEGORY: Date:

| Title : |
| Publisher / Creator : |
| Website / URL : |

Duration: hour(s):   minute(s):

| Timestamp | Takeaway 1 |
| : | |

| Timestamp | Takeaway 2 |
| : | |

| Timestamp | Takeaway 3 |
| : | |

Reflection / Note:

How did the video impact you?

Did it spark any ideas?

Rating

☆ ☆ ☆ ☆ ☆

Timestamp	Takeaway
:	
:	
:	
:	
:	
:	

CATEGORY: Date:

Title :
Publisher / Creator :
Website / URL :

Duration: hour(s):   minute(s):

Timestamp	Takeaway 1

Timestamp	Takeaway 2

Timestamp	Takeaway 3

Reflection / Note:

How did the video impact you?

Did it spark any ideas?

Rating

☆ ☆ ☆ ☆ ☆

Timestamp
Takeaway

Timestamp
Takeaway

Timestamp
Takeaway

Timestamp
Takeaway

Timestamp
Takeaway

Timestamp
Takeaway

CATEGORY: Date:

| Title : |
| Publisher / Creator : |
| Website / URL : |

Duration: hour(s):   minute(s):

| Timestamp | Takeaway 1 |
| : | |

| Timestamp | Takeaway 2 |
| : | |

| Timestamp | Takeaway 3 |
| : | |

Reflection / Note:

How did the video impact you?

Did it spark any ideas?

Rating

Timestamp
Takeaway
:

Timestamp
Takeaway
:

Timestamp
Takeaway
:

Timestamp
Takeaway
:

Timestamp
Takeaway
:

Timestamp
Takeaway
:

CATEGORY: Date:

Title :

Publisher / Creator :

Website / URL :

Duration: hour(s):   minute(s):

Timestamp	Takeaway 1
:	

Timestamp	Takeaway 2
:	

Timestamp	Takeaway 3
:	

Reflection / Note:

How did the video impact you?

Did it spark any ideas?

Rating

Timestamp	Takeaway
:	
:	
:	
:	
:	
:	

CATEGORY
4

CATEGORY:

Date:

Title :

Publisher / Creator :

Website / URL :

Duration: hour(s):   minute(s):

Timestamp

:

Takeaway 1

Timestamp

:

Takeaway 2

Timestamp

:

Takeaway 3

Reflection / Note:

How did the video impact you?

Did it spark any ideas?

Rating

☆ ☆ ☆ ☆ ☆

Timestamp	Takeaway
:	
:	
:	
:	
:	
:	

CATEGORY: Date:

| Title : |
| Publisher / Creator : |
| Website / URL : |

Duration: hour(s):   minute(s):

Timestamp

:

Takeaway 1

Timestamp

:

Takeaway 2

Timestamp

:

Takeaway 3

Reflection / Note:

How did the video impact you?

Did it spark any ideas?

Rating

☆ ☆ ☆ ☆ ☆

Timestamp	Takeaway
:	
:	
:	
:	
:	
:	

CATEGORY: Date:

<table>
<tr><td>Title :</td><td></td></tr>
<tr><td>Publisher / Creator :</td><td></td></tr>
<tr><td>Website / URL :</td><td></td></tr>
</table>

Duration: hour(s):   minute(s):

Timestamp	Takeaway 1
:	

Timestamp	Takeaway 2
:	

Timestamp	Takeaway 3
:	

Reflection / Note:

How did the video impact you?

Did it spark any ideas?

Rating

☆ ☆ ☆ ☆ ☆

Timestamp

Takeaway

:

Timestamp

Takeaway

:

Timestamp

Takeaway

:

Timestamp

Takeaway

:

Timestamp

Takeaway

:

Timestamp

Takeaway

:

CATEGORY: Date:

Title :

Publisher / Creator :

Website / URL :

Duration: hour(s):   minute(s):

Timestamp	Takeaway 1
:	

Timestamp	Takeaway 2
:	

Timestamp	Takeaway 3
:	

Reflection / Note:

How did the video impact you?

Did it spark any ideas?

Rating

Timestamp
Takeaway

Timestamp
Takeaway

Timestamp
Takeaway

Timestamp
Takeaway

Timestamp
Takeaway

Timestamp
Takeaway

CATEGORY: Date:

Duration: hour(s):   minute(s):

Timestamp	Takeaway 1
:	

Timestamp	Takeaway 2
:	

Timestamp	Takeaway 3
:	

Reflection / Note:

How did the video impact you?

Did it spark any ideas?

Rating

Timestamp	Takeaway
:	
:	
:	
:	
:	
:	

CATEGORY: Date:

Title :

Publisher / Creator :

Website / URL :

Duration: hour(s):   minute(s):

Timestamp	Takeaway 1
:	

Timestamp	Takeaway 2
:	

Timestamp	Takeaway 3
:	

Reflection / Note:

How did the video impact you?

Did it spark any ideas?

Rating

☆ ☆ ☆ ☆ ☆

Timestamp
Takeaway
:

Timestamp
Takeaway
:

Timestamp
Takeaway
:

Timestamp
Takeaway
:

Timestamp
Takeaway
:

Timestamp
Takeaway
:

CATEGORY: Date:

| Title : |
| Publisher / Creator : |
| Website / URL : |

Duration: hour(s):   minute(s):

| Timestamp | Takeaway 1 |
| : | |

| Timestamp | Takeaway 2 |
| : | |

| Timestamp | Takeaway 3 |
| : | |

Reflection / Note:

How did the video impact you?

Did it spark any ideas?

Rating

☆ ☆ ☆ ☆ ☆

Timestamp
Takeaway
:

Timestamp
Takeaway
:

Timestamp
Takeaway
:

Timestamp
Takeaway
:

Timestamp
Takeaway
:

Timestamp
Takeaway
:

CATEGORY: Date:

Title :	
Publisher / Creator :	
Website / URL :	

Duration: hour(s):   minute(s):

Timestamp

:

Takeaway 1

Timestamp

:

Takeaway 2

Timestamp

:

Takeaway 3

Reflection / Note:

How did the video impact you?

Did it spark any ideas?

Rating

☆ ☆ ☆ ☆ ☆

Timestamp

Takeaway

:

Timestamp

Takeaway

:

Timestamp

Takeaway

:

Timestamp

Takeaway

:

Timestamp

Takeaway

:

Timestamp

Takeaway

:

CATEGORY: Date:

Title :

Publisher / Creator :

Website / URL :

Duration: hour(s):   minute(s):

Timestamp	Takeaway 1
:	

Timestamp	Takeaway 2
:	

Timestamp	Takeaway 3
:	

Reflection / Note:

How did the video impact you?

Did it spark any ideas?

Rating

☆ ☆ ☆ ☆ ☆

Timestamp	Takeaway
:	
:	
:	
:	
:	
:	

CATEGORY: Date:

Duration: hour(s):   minute(s):

Timestamp	Takeaway 1
:	

Timestamp	Takeaway 2
:	

Timestamp	Takeaway 3
:	

Reflection / Note:

How did the video impact you?

Did it spark any ideas?

Rating

Timestamp	Takeaway
:	
:	
:	
:	
:	
:	

CATEGORY: Date:

<table>
<tr><td>Title :</td><td></td></tr>
<tr><td>Publisher / Creator :</td><td></td></tr>
<tr><td>Website / URL :</td><td></td></tr>
</table>

Duration: hour(s):   minute(s):

Timestamp	Takeaway 1
:	

Timestamp	Takeaway 2
:	

Timestamp	Takeaway 3
:	

Reflection / Note:

How did the video impact you?

Did it spark any ideas?

Rating

Timestamp	Takeaway
:	
:	
:	
:	
:	
:	

CATEGORY: Date:

Title :
Publisher / Creator :
Website / URL :

Duration: hour(s):   minute(s):

| Timestamp | Takeaway 1 |
| : | |

| Timestamp | Takeaway 2 |
| : | |

| Timestamp | Takeaway 3 |
| : | |

Reflection / Note:

How did the video impact you?

Did it spark any ideas?

Rating

Timestamp
Takeaway
Timestamp
Takeaway
Timestamp
Takeaway
Timestamp
Takeaway
Timestamp
Takeaway
Timestamp
Takeaway

CATEGORY: Date:

Title :

Publisher / Creator :

Website / URL :

Duration: hour(s):   minute(s):

Timestamp	Takeaway 1
:	

Timestamp	Takeaway 2
:	

Timestamp	Takeaway 3
:	

Reflection / Note:

How did the video impact you?

Did it spark any ideas?

Rating

☆ ☆ ☆ ☆ ☆

Timestamp	Takeaway
:	
:	
:	
:	
:	
:	

CATEGORY: Date:

Duration: hour(s):   minute(s):

Timestamp	Takeaway 1
:	

Timestamp	Takeaway 2
:	

Timestamp	Takeaway 3
:	

Reflection / Note:

How did the video impact you?

Did it spark any ideas?

Rating

☆ ☆ ☆ ☆ ☆

Timestamp
Takeaway

Timestamp
Takeaway

Timestamp
Takeaway

Timestamp
Takeaway

Timestamp
Takeaway

Timestamp
Takeaway

CATEGORY: Date:

Title :

Publisher / Creator :

Website / URL :

Duration: hour(s):   minute(s):

| Timestamp | Takeaway 1 |
| : | |

| Timestamp | Takeaway 2 |
| : | |

| Timestamp | Takeaway 3 |
| : | |

Reflection / Note:

How did the video impact you?

Did it spark any ideas?

Rating

☆ ☆ ☆ ☆ ☆

Timestamp
Takeaway
:
Timestamp
Takeaway
:
Timestamp
Takeaway
:
Timestamp
Takeaway
:
Timestamp
Takeaway
:
Timestamp
Takeaway
: